C000015454

HARDPRESS.NET
HOME OF HARD-TO-FIND BOOKS

Habit
by William Burns Thomson

Copyright © 2019 by HardPress

Address:
HardPress
8345 NW 66TH ST #2561
MIAMI FL 33166-2626
USA
Email: info@hardpress.net

HABIT:

WITH SPECIAL REFERENCE TO

The Formation of a Virtuous Character.

AN ADDRESS TO STUDENTS,

By BURNS THOMSON.

SECOND EDITION, REVISED.

WITH RECOMMENDATORY NOTE,

By PROFESSOR MILLER.

EDINBURGH:
JOHNSTONE, HUNTER, & CO.

1864.

T.P. 4741

RECOMMENDATORY NOTE

PREFIXED TO FIRST EDITION.

51 QUEEN STREET.

The following ADDRESS was delivered by Mr BURNS THOMSON, Student, at the Annual Meeting of the EDINBURGH UNIVERSITY TEMPERANCE SOCIETY.

It struck the hearers as eminently suited for the occasion, and worthy of a more permanent form than the fleeting words of a mere speech.

Printed with Mr Thomson's consent, it is offered to all Students, with a prayer that God will bless what seems so well calculated to awake and arrest the thoughtless, and to encourage those who have already learned to do well.

JAMES MILLER.

HABIT:

AN ADDRESS TO STUDENTS.

BY ONE OF THEMSELVES.

WE enjoyed the privilege, on a previous occasion, of addressing our fellow-students on this subject, so that what may be said upon it to-night must be regarded as supplementary to a previous address. On the former occasion the subject was viewed almost exclusively with reference to intemperance, and when the same subject was fixed upon again, it was that we might not be limited to intemperance, but might have an opportunity of referring to other matters of interest and importance to which the subject might naturally lead.

Custom is the frequent repetition of an act; habit is the effect produced by that repetition. It is an acquired tendency, proneness, or disposition, to fall into certain states of body or mind, the result of custom. It is not necessary that we should enter into the psychological inquiries respecting its nature, though these are both interesting and important. For the practical purposes we have in view, habit may be regarded as that peculiarity of our constitution by which the present is linked to the past, and in virtue of which we are capable of progress either in good or evil. It is that which strings together the effects of our various activities, and the results of the favourable or unfavourable influences that may be brought to bear upon us. It is that which enables us to calculate upon our fellow-men; which enables us to find each other, and to find ourselves. Were it not for this, which links the present to the future, whatever we may be now, we could have no conception of what we might be on the morrow. Habit may be regarded as holding the place, in the mental and moral, which gravitation holds in the physical world; to this extent, at least, that from a knowledge of the present, we can, in virtue of those laws, with considerable certainty, predict the future. We can not only tell when the sun, moon, or planetary bodies shall suffer an eclipse, but we can predict, with astonishing accuracy, that the profligate spark will soon be eclipsed, if not extinguished, amid the rubbish of what Carlyle so characteristically designates " the ash-bin" of the devil.   With, at least, as much certainty as the meteorologist can predict a fall of rain, hail, or snow, we can predict that the young tippler, who goes swaggering home between two and three in the morning, will soon be vegetating amid the blanching influences of the jail.   It were, therefore, gentlemen, no difficult matter to read your fortunes, not, certainly, as intimating the future of your circumstances, but the future of yourselves.   Your future twelve months hence, or twelve years hence, or millions of years hence, will just be the evolution of the present, plus the effect of the difference of the favourable and unfavourable influences that may bear upon you in the interval.

From these hints respecting the nature of habit, its importance in constituting us what we are, or in the formation of our character, is abundantly clear; for our character may be regarded as the aggregate of our habits.   Taking man as a whole, the character most to be desired is that in which all his faculties are fully and harmoniously developed, in subordination to conscience.   But as at present we cannot view the subject to the extent just indicated, we set aside the consideration of habit in its bearing on the development of the intellect, which might bring us in contact with the *questio vexata* of education, that at present agitates the country; and we shall also dismiss the feelings which only fall indirectly under the laws of habit, and confine ourselves for a moment to the department of desire and volition.   The character most to be desired, in this department, is that in which all the desires work harmoniously together, in due subordination to conscience. The Will gives forth its authoritative word of command, owning the conscience not only to be its legitimate but its actual sovereign. The desires are taught to obey the rein—are habituated to control and subjection,—and they soon learn to submit with cheerfulness to the decision of the will, acting in conformity with the intimations of its master. We are encouraged to the exercise of this self-control, not only from the pleasure which accompanies it, but by the consideration that every time we successfully exercise authority over the desires, we increase our controlling power over them, in consequence of which we can, with greater facility, master them in time to come. If we should neglect to habituate the desires to subordination, they will take the management of affairs into their own hands, and either rule us by turns, or, one of them, by frequent indulgence, may acquire the mastery, and exercise over us a pitiless tyranny. Some there are who will not give themselves the trouble to exercise self-control. When the object of a special desire presents itself, and the longing for its realization is awakened, the will is dragged after the desire, and constrained to adopt measures for its gratification. But, perhaps, when giving the necessary orders for securing the desired end, the object of some other desire makes its appearance, urges its plea, and demands attention. The will is enfeebled—the man is tossed about by every wind. Now, pleasure from one quarter solicits his attention, and he runs; now, it appears in another, and he is turned aside to pursue. In his studies, the beauties of one department of knowledge allure him, and for a day, or perhaps two, he is engaged in their contemplation, when the revelations of some other department of science pass under his notice, and turn him aside. He dabbles in all the branches of knowledge,—he is a proficient in none. "Unstable as water," he cannot excel. Tossed with ceaseless fluctuation, like the waves of the sea, he casts up mire and dirt, and having voluntarily passed *sub jugo*, he is justly given up to the anarchy of desire.

But it may happen, as already hinted, that one desire may be more attended to than the others, and it will requite the attention—like an over-indulged servant—by quietly taking the place of master. The conscience and the will may be so gently and so gradually prepared for the usurpation, that danger is not apprehended—not realized, certainly, on many occasions, till the former is silenced, and the latter made the mere tool and plaything of lust. The tyranny is often terrible and complete. The whole man, body and soul, is compelled to labour for the gratification of one dominant passion. The noblest faculties of human nature are made to act the part of hewers of wood and drawers of water, to minister to its satisfaction. And just as the simpleton, who has taught his servant to leave her position of due subordination, comes to be rebuked for impertinence when he would establish proper relations, and is sometimes glad to smooth-up matters by the bestowal of a gift, so it often happens, when the conscience ventures to demur to

existing arrangements, and hints at the propriety
of establishing a better order of things, that its
mutterings of disapprobation are the prelude to an
unusual indulgence, as if the offended usurper would
compel her to do penance for venturing to question
the legitimacy of his control. This suggests a
thought respecting the feelings that requires ex-
plicit notice, as tending to bring out the helpless-
ness of the victim of a predominating propensity.
Were it possible for the drunkard, for example, to
regard intemperance with the moral disapprobation
with which he viewed it before he fell under its
power, then, those moral emotions awaking their
suitable desires, there might be motive power exer-
cised over the will sufficient to counterbalance the
influence resulting from his vicious habits; but,
alas! as the propensity grows strong, the feelings
which might have operated with a counteracting
influence grow weak, so that the wretched being is
doubly cursed—cursed in the strengthening of the
impulsive tendency to evil, and in the weakening
of the influences that restrain from vice.

The bearing of these truths we traced at considerable length on a previous evening in reference
to drunkenness, and gave many illustrative cases.
With a single specimen of the effects of the drinking usages, we shall pass to other dangers that
beset the student, leaving you to follow out for
yourselves the bearing of the principles just stated
on what we can bring under your notice only in
the form of general observations.

Entering college one day I saw a man dressed
in black, with a white neckerchief, holding on by

the gate. He recognised me, and, drunk as he
was, he shrunk back into the corner at the Post-
office.   Standing on the stair at the quadrangle, I
awaited the students of my acquaintance, who were
not abstainers, and laying hold of them as they
came up, read them a lecture to the following effect :
—" You see that man staggering at the gate? That
man is the son of a minister, whose published ser-
mons are read with interest and profit,—that man
attended 'a literary and theological course at the
University,—that man was one of the first classical
scholars in town,—that man has preached the gospel in this very city,—that man has been several
times in prison for dishonesty. Now, there he
stands! the victim of the drinking usages of society."
The practical application of this discourse was left
with themselves—it is now left with you.

It were certainly to convey an impression very
remote from the truth, were intemperance repre-
sented as the only danger to which students are exposed, or that drinking usage is the only influence
hostile to virtue from which they are liable to suffer in passing through their curriculum. For though
it be true that drink has slain its thousands, it is
not less true that the theatre and gambling have
slain their tens of thousands. It were easy to give
two cases in which the theatre and gambling have,
directly or indirectly, effected the ruin of students,
for one in which it has been accomplished solely by
drink. The distance between Shakespeare Square
and the Calton—between the Theatre and the
Jail—is, in every sense, very short. Adopting
the language of those who have been its victims,

there is a tendency in the theatre to place them in an ideal world, and to give them a distaste for the commonplace duties of life,—to transform them into the heroes of the night,—in consequence of which they become impatient of control, fret under the just rebukes of an injured father, and even loathe the pathetic pleadings of a mother's tears. The admonitions which might be suitable to a son are not at all suitable when addressed to a hero. The youth is changed; he is not the same person as before; he may leave home in the evening a child, and return at night a stranger. From a home which his vitiated tastes has rendered insipid, if not intolerable,—from an authority against whose exercise he secretly repines, if he do not openly rebel, —and from an affection whose expression is like wormwood to his heart, he turns to seek sympathy in companionships more congenial to his depraved tastes. The difficulty in obtaining means to gratify the desire of witnessing the drama often leads to dishonesty. The mind occupies itself with schemes, utterly inconsistent with rectitude, for replenishing the purse; and the consequent familiarity in thought with that which is base and dishonest, lowers the tone of the moral sentiments, and paves the way to practices which sometimes land even students in imprisonment or exile. At the close of the play there are strong temptations to partake of a little "*refreshment*," which not only exposes to the danger of forming or fostering another ruinous habit, but the resulting stimulus to the system, combined with the effect of what, during the evening, he had heard and seen, mightily increases his liability to fall a victim to another evil which encircles the theatre, and besets him on his way home. Conversing on this subject, in prison, with one who knew it well,—the son of a preacher of the gospel, —it was remarked that some people thought the theatre a splendid place. "Yes," he said, "it is a splendid place,—it is a splendid emporium of vice, —it is a splendid place for ruining youth,—a splendid place for filling *houses* with victims and with villains; and a most splendid short cut to the jail."

Another danger to which we are exposed, but which we can merely mention, is gambling. At the end of the class hour we are lugged off by a companion to the billiard-room to get a little amusement. We never think of betting, and at first we are not asked. The "decoy ducks" simply arrange, when we have begun to acquire a liking for the play, that the party losing shall be at the expense of a little "refreshment." This forms an excellent stepping-stone to betting in a more definite form. It adds somewhat to the excitement of the game, and as the stake is paltry, that excitement is pleasurable, which, of course, increases our desire for a repetition of the amusement, and so the gambling propensity developes itself. There is also a strong temptation, during the game, to sip the brandy and water which too commonly circulates around the board. And we are thus exposed to dangers from which few if any escape; for either we fall into the habits of the confirmed gambler, or into those of the confirmed drunkard, or we accelerate our ruin by falling victims to both.

There are yet other dangers than those adverted

to that beset us, which bear upon us specially as students.   They are seldom spoken of; we experience little if any sympathy in the mental struggles to which they frequently give rise; their danger is little apprehended, even though some promising youth is ever and anon blighted by their withering influence, turned aside from his course, and cast adrift amid the blank desolations of scepticism. The collective utterance of not a few of the subjects of study with which we are expected to be conversant is, that man is irresponsible; and individually, how many of our Philosophies whisper in the ear of the young inquirer,—" Walk in the light of your own eyes, betake yourselves to the gin-shop, the theatre, and the billiard-room; follow the desires of your own heart, for man is irresponsible!" When, by persevering and earnest application, we have reached the last generalization of Transcendentalism, and find ourselves full in front of a Μη 'Ον, or an absolute negation, all around is so empty, so cold, so abstract, so impersonal, that we hear,—alas! there is nothing to be heard in those infinite solitudes but the quickened palpitation of our own unsatisfied hearts,—but we *feel* the deliverance of spiritualism sinking like a death-chill to the centre of our being—man is irresponsible!   Pantheism appears, and brings near the God that was afar off, but it brings no influence more favourable to the promotion of virtue.   It gives the realization of the promise, " Ye shall be God," for it transmutes us into Deity, and Deity into us.   We are really and truly bits of God; our faults and errors are the actings of Divinity, and our conscious self-condemnations are the voice of God. How unmistakeable its utterance: "It is impossible to err; God cannot sin! Man is God—God is man! Students! do as you please—man is irresponsible!" Materialism lays its cold hand upon us, and by its magic touch would transform us into blocks, and stones, and worse than senseless things. Nor is it only in the seclusion of the college, or in the privacy of our own apartment, that it meets us. In our Halls of Philosophy it presents itself in its grossest form, and coolly tells us that we are nothing but lumps of living granite: "Animated chlorine knows of chlorine; incarnate zinc of zinc; and all that is yet inanimate will one day speak and reason."* We need not wonder if, at no distant period, the Calton Hill, tired of its inactivity, should break up, and its molecules, perhaps, according to some pre-established harmony, should develope themselves into the Abercrombies and Alisons, the Chalmerses and the Guthries, of a coming age, who would doubtless rejoice to act the part of benefactors to their fellow-lumps of vitalised porphyry and living quartz. How clear and unequivocal the tendency of such a system—"Let us eat, drink, and be merry, for to-morrow we die"—man is irresponsible. Okenism, too, by degrading our origin, would sever every tie that binds us to the Creator, and destroy those indefinite longings of the human heart after re-attachment to Deity, which impart dignity to humanity, even in its ruins. It would drag us down amid the mud and slime which encircles the

---

* See Emerson's "Representative Men."

emerging Himalayas, and, transfusing through us galvanic currents, would vitalise us, and send us up through plants and animals to man.   It conducts us from the sea froth—through sea plants and sea animals, through reptiles, birds, mammals, and introduces us to our professors, "monkeys minus the tail."   Man at best is but a superior kind of brute—man is irresponsible.   Nor is the medical student without influences unfavourable to virtue in his peculiar field of inquiry.   In his physiological investigations he soon reaches the constituents of tissue—cells, nuclei, and nucleoli; he sees cell develope itself within cell, in apparently endless succession; he sees the spermatozoa moving about like tadpoles, which only require conditions favourable to the development and agglomeration of cells for perfecting the human organism; and when chemistry tells him that vitality is as much a property of oxygen as is its property of forming acids with various other elements, and when it combines in given proportion with certain of these elements, vitality as naturally results as oil of vitriol from the union of certain proportions of oxygen and sulphur, —the tendency is, and the effect sometimes actually is, to land the student in an eternal generative series,—in the Positivism of Comte,—in the materiality of the soul.   How much do we meet with in the prosecution of our studies calculated to weaken our sense of responsibility, and which exerts over us a silent, but sometimes powerful influence, hostile to the formation and development of a virtuous character!

Permit me now, gentlemen, to call attention to a truth which imparts vast additional significance and force to what has been said respecting the dangers and unfavourable influences that encompass us. It is the truth, that just as invariably as the tiger cub developes into a treacherous and bloodthirsty animal, man grows up a consciously erring, a consciously guilty creature. There is evidently a natural bent or bias predisposing to that which is wrong. This bias evolves itself in action of the same character with itself: the action operates reflexly, and strengthens the disposition from which it flowed; and thus practice and principle, acting and re-acting upon each other, and mutually affecting each other in accordance with the laws of our nature, we grow up habituated to modes of thought and action not only vicious in themselves, but which increase, to an inconceivable extent, the power over us, for evil, of the various influences referred to above. To what, gentlemen, have we been accustoming ourselves? Why, during our lifetime we have accustomed ourselves to trifle with the deliverances of conscience—to trifle with the deliverances of God; and it is impossible we could habituate ourselves to such trifling with Deity without lowering our conceptions of His majesty, which at once clears the way for the indulgence of vicious propensity, and diminishes the incitements to virtue. Such custom, at the same time, necessarily lowers our conception of the majesty of the divine law written on the heart,—it lowers our conception of the exceeding moral turpitude of even the slightest deviation from the law of moral rectitude,—it lowers our conception of the necessity of an atoning work without, and an almighty work within, in order to set us right,—it lowers our conception of the glory of the abodes of perfect virtue, the contemplation of which should allure us from vice, for they are the dwelling-place of a paltry God,—it lowers our conception of the terribleness of the place of misery, the thought of which should deter us from vice, for it is a place for the punishment of paltry sin,—till we are lowered amid the tremendous realities of eternity, bundles of vicious habits.

Shall it be thought presumptuous on the part of a fellow-student, in view of what has been said, to call attention to the means—the only means—of begetting and developing a truly virtuous character? We do not dream of interfering with your course of study; we would not ask you to forsake the company of Socrates, or to desert the hallowed groves of Academe; but we do venture to call attention to One whose necessity Socrates demonstrated, and whose probable appearance heathen philosophy ventured to predict. Nor would we ask you to renounce the society of Plato; nay, rather, with feeble pinion, let us strive to reach those heights where the divine philosopher habitually soared, contemplating the perfections of Deity; but let us ever and anon descend, and sit—like little children sit—at the feet of Him in whom dwelt the fulness of the Godhead bodily. Philosophy may acquaint us with our needs, but she cannot supply them. She tells us it is our duty to elevate ourselves in the scale of moral being by every means consistent with rectitude; but the best means she can provide are inadequate even to give us the start in the paths of genuine virtue. Contact with the best that humanity can furnish is contact with imperfection, and the reflex effect of such contact is an imperfection greater than the original. We would require, in order to set us agoing, and to keep us agoing, in the ways of true virtue, a perfect precept, a perfect pattern, and an almighty power. Virtuous habits are to be begun and developed, not by companionship with the son of Sophroniscus, but by companionship with the Son of Mary. It is only by living, personal, and continued contact with Him, that we can acquire a truly virtuous character. In His society, virtue should not only be begun, but be " perfected, stablished, strengthened, and settled;" its expansion and development would be like the path of the shining light, shining more and more unto the perfect day, and we should ultimately enter eternity to enjoy its blessed rewards. · And the hope, gentlemen, of reaching a state where dangers and hostile influences are for ever unknown,— the hope that, at no distant period, we may be tenanting the abodes of perfect virtue,—would fill us with intensest longing for the possession of those habits that render suitable for the realms of light; and, on such a pleasant occasion as the present, what can be more pleasant than the thought that we,—even we ourselves,—when all the trials of our virtue are past, and our characters are like the character of Him who is altogether lovely, may be permitted to re-assemble in a better land, where, with expanded capacities, and expanded capabilities, in perfect peace, in fulness of joy, we may sit

anew at the feet of our professors, and learn a pro-
founder science than they can at present impart;
yea, with our professors we may range throughout
eternity amid the treasures of Infinite Wisdom and
Love!

C. GIBSON, PRINTER, THISTLE STREET, EDINBURGH.

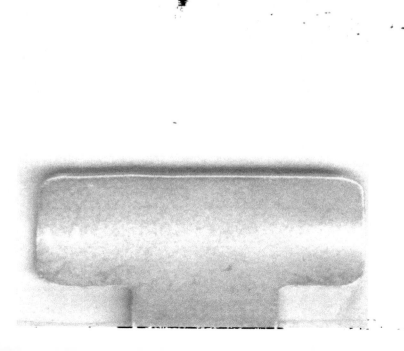

Check Out More Titles From HardPress Classics Series In
this collection we are offering thousands of classic and hard
to find books. This series spans a vast array of subjects – so
you are bound to find something of interest to enjoy reading
and learning about.

Subjects:
Architecture
Art
Biography & Autobiography
Body, Mind &Spirit
Children & Young Adult
Dramas
Education
Fiction
History
Language Arts & Disciplines
Law
Literary Collections
Music
Poetry
Psychology
Science
…and many more.

Visit us at www.hardpress.net

Im TheStory
personalised classic books

"Beautiful gift.. lovely finish.
My Niece loves it, so precious!"

Helen R Brumfieldon

⭐⭐⭐⭐⭐

UNIQUE GIFT

FOR KIDS, PARTNERS
AND FRIENDS

Timeless books such as:

Kids

Alice in Wonderland · The Jungle Book · The Wonderful Wizard of Oz
Peter and Wendy · Robin Hood · The Prince and The Pauper
The Railway Children · Treasure Island · A Christmas Carol

Adults

Romeo and Juliet · Dracula

Highly Customizable **Change** Books Title **Replace** Characters Names with yours **Upload** Photo for its de page **Add** Inscriptions

Visit
Im TheStory.com
and order yours today!

Lightning Source UK Ltd.
Milton Keynes UK
UKHW020631110520
363086UK00012B/1089